COOKING
SALADS

FOR
BEGINNERS

Jamie Romier

Table of Contents

COLORFUL MEANS HEALTHY 7

Autumn Duck Confit Salad.............................. 8

Balsamic Vinegar Potato Salad.......................... 11

Beet Salad With Goat Cheese 13

Bocconcini Salad.....................................16

Bulgur Chickpea Salad................................18

California Cherry And Walnut Salad 20

Caprese Salad With Balsamic Reduction..................... 22

Cashew Curry Spinach Salad........................... 25

Cherry Chicken Salad 29

Chicken Salad With Couscous.........................31

Conch Salad.. 34

Couscous Feta Salad 37

Asparagus And Pancetta Salad...................... 40

Antipasto Salad 43

Apple, Avocado And Hearts Of Palm Salad 46

Apple Cranberry Salad 48

Arugula Persimmon Pear Salad 50

Arugula Salad With Citrus Vinaigrette 52

Cranberry Pecan Salad 54

Cucumber Mango Salad With Citrus Vinaigrette 57

Dandelion Salad 60

Denise Salad Number One 62

Detox Salad 64

Easy Arugula Salad 66

Green Apple Salad With Blueberries, Feta, And Walnuts
.... 68

Green Mango Salad 70

Green Salad With Cranberry Vinaigrette 72

Grilled Panzanella Salad With Peaches And Fennel 74

Grilled Romaine Salad 78

Ham And Swiss Salad With Red Currants 81

Hot Chicken Liver And Fennel Salad 83

Jarjeer (Arugula) Salad 86

Eggplant Salad With Feta And Pomegranate 88

Elegant Brunch Chicken Salad 90

Roasted Vegetable Salad... 93

Ensalada De Nopales (Mexican Cactus Salad) 96

Escarole Siciliano... 99

Fall Salad With Quinoa, Brussels Sprouts, And
Pomegranate 101

Fennel And Orange Salad.. 104

French Lentil Salad With Goat Cheese 106

Fresh Avocado Burrata Salad 109

Gabe's Coffee Crusted Hanger Steak With Apple,
Fennel, And Herb Salad..111

Mango Papaya Salad.. 116

Mandarin Orange Salad... 119

Gourmet Tuna Salad...122

Calamari Salad 124

Greek Pasta Salad With Roasted Vegetables And Feta
....126

THANK YOU..129

COLORFUL MEANS HEALTHY

Autumn Duck Confit Salad

Serving: 2

Ingredients

Salad:

- 2 cooked duck confit legs (with thighs attached)
- 1 cup curly endive (frisee)
- 1 cup arugula
- 1 cup chopped radicchio
- 1/2 cup purple grapes
- 1/2 cup peeled and minced apple
- 1/4 cup thinly sliced white turnip
- 1/4 cup coarsely chopped pecans

Dressing:

- 3 tablespoons olive oil
- 1 tablespoon maple syrup
- 1 tablespoon red wine vinegar
- salt and ground black pepper to taste

Direction

- Preheat the oven to 350°F (175°C) Put the duck on a baking tray.

- Cook in the oven for 7 minutes, until heated through.

- Combine arugula, curly endive, grapes, turnip, apple, radicchio, and pecans in a big bowl.

- Toss in maple syrup, salt, pepper, olive oil, and vinegar in a bowl. Whisk it and pour over the salad. Mix well to coat every ingredient.

- Divide the salad into two bowls. Top salad with duck confit.

Nutrition Information

- Calories: 425 calories;

- Total Fat: 33.9

- Sodium: 138

- Total Carbohydrate: 23.6

- Cholesterol: 33

- Protein: 10.5

Balsamic Vinegar Potato Salad

Serving: 8

Ingredients

- 10 medium red potatoes, diced
- 1 small onion, chopped
- 1/2 cup diced roasted red peppers
- 1 (4 ounce) can sliced black olives, drained
- 1 (10 ounce) can quartered artichoke hearts, drained
- 1/2 cup balsamic vinegar
- 3 teaspoons olive oil
- 1 teaspoon dried oregano
- 1 teaspoon dried basil
- 1/2 teaspoon mustard powder

- 2 tablespoons chopped fresh parsley

Direction

- Cover potatoes with enough water in a saucepan. Boil then cook till tender, for 5-10 minutes. Let drain and move to a large bowl.

- Add artichokes, olives, red peppers and onion to the potatoes bowl. Whisk together parsley, mustard powder, basil, oregano, olive oil and balsamic vinegar in a separate bowl. Spread over the vegetables and stir till coated. Before serving, let chill for at least 4 hours to overnight.

Nutrition Information

- Calories: 257 calories;

- Total Fat: 3.9

- Sodium: 407

- Total Carbohydrate: 51.1

- Cholesterol: 0

- Protein: 6.9

Beet Salad With Goat Cheese

Serving: 6

Ingredients

- 4 medium beets - scrubbed, trimmed and cut in half

- 1/3 cup chopped walnuts

- 3 tablespoons maple syrup

- 1 (10 ounce) package mixed baby salad greens

- 1/2 cup frozen orange juice concentrate

- 1/4 cup balsamic vinegar

- 1/2 cup extra-virgin olive oil

- 2 ounces goat cheese

Direction

- Cover beets with enough water in saucepan; boil. Cook till tender for 20-30 minutes. Drain; cool. Cut to cubes.

- Put walnuts in skillet on medium low heat as beets cook; heat till beginning to toast and warm; mix maple syrup in. Mix and cook till coated evenly; take off heat. Put aside; cool.

- Whisk olive oil, balsamic vinegar and orange juice concentrate in small bowl for dressing.

- On each of 4 salad plates, put big helping of baby greens; evenly divide candied walnuts then sprinkle on greens. Put even amount of beets on greens; put dabs of goat cheese on top. Drizzle some dressing on each plate.

Nutrition Information

- Calories: 347 calories;

- Protein: 5.3

- Total Fat: 26.1

- Sodium: 107

- Total Carbohydrate: 25

- Cholesterol: 7

Bocconcini Salad

Ingredients

- 1 pound bocconcini (bite-size mozzarella balls)
- 8 cherry tomatoes, halved
- 1/2 cup chopped green bell pepper
- 1/2 cup chopped celery
- 1/2 cup Belgian endive leaves
- 1/2 cup coarsely chopped arugula, stems included
- 1 1/2 tablespoons fresh lemon juice
- 3 tablespoons extra virgin olive oil
- 2 tablespoons chopped fresh basil leaves
- salt and freshly ground black pepper

Direction

Combine arugula, endive, celery, bell pepper, cherry tomatoes and mozzarella in a large salad bowl.

Add olive oil and lemon juice together, whisk properly then pour over the salad. Toss well in order that all ingredients are well coated with dressing. Move salad to individual serving plates if needed. Sprinkle basil on top of salad; add salt and pepper to season, serve immediately.

Nutrition Information

- Calories: 448 calories;

- Total Fat: 35.7

- Sodium: 875

- Total Carbohydrate: 6.2

- Cholesterol: 90

- Protein: 25.9

Bulgur Chickpea Salad

Serving: 7

Ingredients

- 1 cup bulgur

- 2 cups boiling water

- 1/2 cup vegetable oil

- 1/2 cup fresh lemon juice

- salt to taste

- ground black pepper to taste

- 1 cup chopped green onions

- 1 (15 ounce) can garbanzo beans, drained

- 1 cup chopped fresh parsley

- 1 cup grated carrots

Direction

- Prepare a heatproof bowl, add in bulgur, and pour boiling water over bulgur. Allow to stand for 1 hour at room temperature.

- Beat together pepper, salt, lemon juice, and oil in a small bowl. Pour the mixture over bulgur, use a fork to mix properly.

- In a nice glass serving bowl, place bulgur in the bottom. On top of the bulgur, place layers of garbanzo beans and vegetables in this order: green onions, garbanzo beans, parsley, and carrots on top. Cover the bowl, put in the refrigerator to keep cold. Toss well just before serving

Nutrition Information

Calories: 273 calories;

Protein: 5.2

Total Fat: 16.6

California Cherry And Walnut Salad

Serving: 4

Ingredients

- 1 (10 ounce) bag mixed salad greens
- 1/4 cup raspberry vinaigrette
- 1/4 cup walnut pieces
- 2 tablespoons dried tart cherries
- 4 ounces goat cheese, sliced
- 1/4 pound cooked chicken breast strips

Direction

- In a large bowl, add dried cherries, walnut pieces, raspberry vinaigrette and salad greens, toss until well mixed. Distribute salad into individual salad plates or bowls. Decorate each salad with few chicken breast strips and two slices of goat cheese.

Nutrition Information

- Calories: 254 calories;

- Sodium: 401

- Total Carbohydrate: 13.4

- Cholesterol: 44

- Protein: 16.5

- Total Fat: 15.6

Caprese Salad With Balsamic Reduction

Serving: 4

Ingredients

- 1 cup balsamic vinegar

- 1/4 cup honey

- 3 large tomatoes, cut into 1/2-inch slices

- 1 (16 ounce) package fresh mozzarella cheese, cut into 1/4-inch slices

- 1/4 teaspoon salt

- 1/4 teaspoon ground black pepper

- 1/2 cup fresh basil leaves

- 1/4 cup extra-virgin olive oil

Direction

- In a small saucepan, stir together honey and balsamic vinegar, place saucepan over high heat. Bring mixture to a boil, lower the heat to low and simmer for about 10 minutes or until the amount of vinegar mixture decreases to 1/3 cup. Set aside the balsamic reduction and allow it to cool.

- On a serving platter, lay out mozzarella cheese and slices of tomatoes decoratively. Add salt and black pepper to season, put fresh basil leaves on top of the salad, and drizzle salad with balsamic reduction and olive oil.

Nutrition Information

Calories: 580 calories;

Total Fat: 38.8

Sodium: 331

Total Carbohydrate: 34.8

Cholesterol: 89

Protein: 22

Cashew Curry Spinach Salad

Serving: 6

Ingredients

- Dressing:

- 1/2 cup vegetable oil

- 3 tablespoons red wine vinegar

- 3 tablespoons Dijon mustard

- 3 tablespoons sesame seeds

- 2 tablespoons honey

- 1 teaspoon chopped garlic

- Salad:

- 1/2 pound bacon

- 12 cups spinach leaves

- 6 cups coarsely chopped frisee (French curly endive)
- 3 small pears, thinly sliced
- 2/3 red onion, thinly sliced
- 6 grapes, halved (optional)
- Cashews:
- 3/4 cup raw cashews
- 1 tablespoon butter
- 1 tablespoon brown sugar
- 1 teaspoon curry powder
- 1 teaspoon dried rosemary
- 1/2 teaspoon salt
- 1/8 teaspoon cayenne pepper

Direction

- To make dressing, mix together garlic, honey, sesame seeds, Dijon mustard, red wine vinegar and vegetable oil in a bowl.

- In a large skillet, place in bacon and cook over medium-high heat, flip occasionally for about 10 minutes until turn brown evenly. Put bacon slices on paper towel to drain. Crumble into small pieces.

- On an individual serving plates, layer bacon crumbles, spinach leaves, frisee, pears, red onion, and grapes.

- Set oven to 400°F (200°C) and start preheating. Spread cashews evenly on a baking sheet.

- In a saucepan, melt butter over low heat. Add in cayenne pepper, salt, rosemary, curry powder and brown sugar, stir well until the mixture is smooth.

- In the preheated oven, toast cashew for 8 to 10 minutes until turn lightly brown. Add in cashew to the saucepan with butter mixture; stir until well coated. Allow to cool for about 10 minutes. Add cashew in salad plates, drizzle dressing over and serve

Nutrition Information

Calories: 481 calories;

Total Fat: 35.7

Sodium: 746

Total Carbohydrate: 33.9

Cholesterol: 19

Protein: 11.5

Cherry Chicken Salad

Serving: 4

Ingredients

- 3 cooked, boneless chicken breast halves, diced
- 1/3 cup dried cherries
- 1/3 cup diced celery
- 1/3 cup toasted, chopped pecans
- 1/3 cup low-fat mayonnaise
- 1 tablespoon buttermilk
- 1/2 teaspoon salt
- 1/2 teaspoon ground black pepper
- 1/3 cup cubed apples (optional)

Direction

- Mix chicken, pepper, dried cherries, salt, celery, milk, nuts, and mayonnaise together in a big bowl.

- Apple can be added as well if desired.

- Combine together and place in the refrigerator until cold.

- Serve salad with croissants or toasted cracked wheat bread.

Nutrition Information

- Calories: 264 calories;

- Sodium: 356

- Total Carbohydrate: 12

- Cholesterol: 62

- Protein: 24.3

- Total Fat: 12.7

Chicken Salad With Couscous

Serving: 6

Ingredients

- 1 cup couscous

- 2 cups chicken broth

- 1/2 cup dry white wine

- 2 teaspoons olive oil

- 2 tablespoons fresh lime juice

- 1 1/2 teaspoons ground cumin

- 1 clove garlic, minced

- 1 pound skinless, boneless chicken breast meat - cubed

- 1 green bell pepper, cut into large chunks

- 1 red bell pepper, cut into large chunks

- 1 yellow bell pepper, cut into large chunks
- 4 green onions, chopped
- 1/4 cup pitted black olives

Direction

- Prepare couscous pasta based on package directions, use chicken broth for the liquid. Drain off and set aside.
- Combine garlic, 1 teaspoon cumin, 1 tablespoon lime juice, oil and wine in a large skillet, mix well, and put in chicken. Set the heat to low to simmer for 5 to 7 minutes or until chicken juices run clear and all liquid fully evaporates.
- Move chicken from the skillet to a large bowl, add couscous, green onion, yellow bell pepper, red bell pepper, green bell pepper, leftover 1 tablespoon lime juice and remaining 1/2 teaspoon cumin, mix well. Decorate per serving with few black olives.

Nutrition Information

- Calories: 281 calories;
- Protein: 25.9

- Total Fat: 4.5

- Sodium: 633

- Total Carbohydrate: 29.5

- Cholesterol: 45

Conch Salad

Serving: 8

Ingredients

- 1 pound fresh conch
- 1 1/4 cups lemon juice, divided
- 1 cup diced tomatoes
- 1/2 cup diced onion
- 1/2 cup diced green bell pepper
- 1/2 cup diced cucumber
- 1/4 teaspoon seasoning blend (such as Badia® Complete Seasoning®), or to taste
- 1 pinch seasoned salt, or to taste
- 2 cups tomato juice
- 1/4 cup lime juice
- 1/4 cup vinegar
- 1 dash hot sauce, or to taste

Direction

- Use meat mallet to tenderized conch. Cut into bite-size pieces. Prepare 1 cup of lemon juice, add in conch to soak for at least 2 hours, better if soak overnight.

- Remove conch from lemon juice and place in a bowl. Add in seasoned salt, seasoning blend, cucumber, green pepper, onion and tomatoes, mix well.

- Move conch mixture to a container. Add in lime juice, tomato juice and remaining of 1/4 cup lemon juice, mix properly. Add in hot sauce and vinegar, stir well. Put in the refrigerator and keep cold for about 1 hour until the flavors are well combined. Serve cold

Nutrition Information

- Calories: 111 calories;

- Protein: 14.6

- Sodium: 320

- Total Carbohydrate: 13.5

- Cholesterol: 37

- Total Fat: 0.3

Couscous Feta Salad

Serving: 8

Ingredients

- 2 cups water

- 1 1/3 cups couscous

- 1 teaspoon salt

- 1/2 teaspoon ground black pepper

- 2 tablespoons red wine vinegar

- 1 1/2 tablespoons Dijon mustard

- 1/2 cup olive oil

- 1 cucumber, seeded and chopped

- 1 (4 ounce) container crumbled feta cheese

- 6 green onions, chopped

- 1/2 cup chopped fresh parsley

- 1/4 cup toasted pine nuts

Direction

- Boil water in a saucepan over high heat. Remove it from the heat. Mix in couscous. Cover the pan and allow it to stand for 10 minutes. Scrape the couscous into the mixing bowl. Use a fork to fluff the couscous. Refrigerate it for 1 hour until cold.

- Make the dressing once the couscous is cold by mixing the red wine vinegar, Dijon mustard, salt, and black pepper in a small bowl. Drizzle in olive oil slowly while mixing the mixture until the oil has thickened the dressing. Fold in feta cheese, pine nuts, parsley, cucumber, and green onions into the couscous. Pour the dressing all over the top and mix until evenly moistened. Before serving, let the mixture chill first for 30 minutes.

Nutrition Information

- Calories: 304 calories;
- Total Fat: 18.9
- Sodium: 528
- Total Carbohydrate: 26.8
- Cholesterol: 13

Asparagus And Pancetta Salad

Serving: 8

Ingredients

- 2 pounds asparagus, trimmed

- 4 tablespoons extra-virgin olive oil, divided

- 2 cloves garlic, minced

- 1/4 pound pancetta, cut crosswise into 1/8 inch sticks

- 3 tablespoons lemon juice

- 2 teaspoons Dijon mustard

Direction

- Fill a steamer with 1 inch of boiling water so that the asparagus is soaked in it. Let the asparagus cook for 2-6 minutes until it is soft yet still firm. Drain the cooked asparagus and place it in a bowl of ice water to let it cool down; place the cooled down cooked asparagus on paper towers to drain excess liquid then put it on the serving platter.

- Put 1 tablespoon of olive oil in a medium-sized saucepan placed on medium-low heat and let it heat up. Put in the garlic and sauté it in hot oil for 2-3 minutes until you can already smell the aroma. Put in the pancetta and keep cooking for 8-10 minutes while stirring until it turns brown in color.

- Move the pan away from heat and mix the lemon juice, Dijon and leftover 3 tablespoons of olive oil into the pancetta mixture. Drizzle the prepared sauce on top of the asparagus.

Nutrition Information

- Calories: 113 calories;

- Cholesterol: 5

- Protein: 4.3

- Total Fat: 8.8

- Sodium: 142

- Total Carbohydrate: 5.5

Antipasto Salad

Ingredients

- 8 ounces Genoa salami, cut into bite-size pieces

- 8 ounces sopressata or other hard salami, cut into bite-size pieces

- 8 ounces sharp provolone cheese, cut into bite-size pieces

- 8 ounces fresh mozzarella cheese, cut into bite-size pieces

- 2 large tomatoes, cut into bite-size pieces

- 1 (14 ounce) can artichokes, drained and cut into bite-size pieces

- 1/2 (12 ounce) jar roasted red peppers, drained and sliced

- 1/2 cup pitted and coarsely chopped Kalamata olives

- 1/4 cup pitted and chopped green olives

- 1 tablespoon extra-virgin olive oil

- 3 tablespoons red wine vinegar

- freshly-ground black pepper, to taste

- 1/4 cup shredded fresh basil leaves

Direction

- Mix artichokes, tomatoes, mozzarella, provolone, sopressata salami and Genoa in a bowl. Slice roasted red peppers; add in the bowl with 3 tablespoons of the juice.

- Mix chopped olives in; drizzle olive oil on the whole dish then black pepper and red wine vinegar. You can prepare salad ahead of time then refrigerate till serving.

- Tear fresh basil leaves to bite-sized pieces; add to salad before serving. Mix well; serve.

Nutrition Information

- Calories: 383 calories;

- Sodium: 1783

- Total Carbohydrate: 7.9

- Cholesterol: 74

- Protein: 21.7

- Total Fat: 29.1

Apple, Avocado And Hearts Of Palm Salad

Serving: 6

Ingredients

- 1 cup mayonnaise
- 1/4 cup ketchup
- 1 tablespoon white sugar
- 1 lemon, juiced
- 1/4 teaspoon paprika
- 1 pinch ground black pepper
- 2 tablespoons chopped fresh chives
- 3 cups mixed salad greens
- 1 avocado - pitted, peeled, and cubed
- 2 Granny Smith apples - peeled, cored and sliced thin
- 1/2 cup coarsely chopped walnuts
- 1 cup sliced hearts of palm

Direction

- Whisk pepper, paprika, lemon juice, sugar, ketchup and mayonnaise together in a small bowl. Add chives, stir well and set aside.
- On individual serving plates, lay out the watercress. Place hearts of palm, avocado and apple on top. Add walnuts on top and sprinkle with dressing.
- Drizzle the dressing evenly over salad and serve.

Nutrition Information

- Calories: 435 calories;
- Sodium: 434
- Total Carbohydrate: 19.5
- Cholesterol: 14
- Protein: 4.1
- Total Fat: 40.8

Apple Cranberry Salad

Serving: 4

Ingredients

- 1 teaspoon stone-ground mustard
- 2 tablespoons balsamic vinegar
- 1/4 cup olive oil
- 1 apple, diced
- 1 pear, diced
- 1/4 cup dried cranberries
- 1 (10 ounce) package mixed baby greens
- 1/4 cup crumbled blue cheese
- 2 tablespoons chopped walnuts

Direction

- In a small bowl, whisk together vinegar and mustard; while whisking, sprinkle in the olive oil to make a dressing; set aside.

- In a large salad bowl, put walnuts, blue cheese, baby greens, cranberries, pear and apple. Mix by tossing gently, pour dressing over salad, and toss until well coated.

Nutrition Information

- Calories: 256 calories;

- Total Fat: 18.6

- Sodium: 160

- Total Carbohydrate: 21.5

- Cholesterol: 6

- Protein: 3.7

Arugula Persimmon Pear Salad

Serving: 2

Ingredients

- 1 teaspoon Dijon mustard
- 1/2 lemon, juiced
- 1/4 cup olive oil
- 1 shallot, minced
- 1 persimmon, sliced
- 1 pear, sliced
- 1/2 cup walnut pieces, toasted
- 1 bunch arugula
- 1 tablespoon shaved Parmesan cheese
- salt and pepper to taste

Direction

- Mix shallot, olive oil, lemon juice, and mustard in a bowl. Add arugula, walnuts, pear, and sliced persimmon and mix it well until coated.

- Top salad with shaved parmesan cheese and season with pepper and salt.

Nutrition Information

- Calories: 527 calories;

- Protein: 9.3

- Total Fat: 45.1

- Sodium: 140

- Total Carbohydrate: 30.7

- Cholesterol: 2

Arugula Salad With Citrus Vinaigrette

Serving: 4

Ingredients

- 1/3 cup freshly squeezed grapefruit juice

- 1/3 cup freshly squeezed orange juice

- 1/3 cup extra virgin olive oil

- salt to taste

- 6 ounces arugula - rinsed, dried and torn

- 1 pear, cored and sliced

- 1 red bell pepper, thinly sliced

Direction

- Mix salt, grapefruit juice, olive oil, and orange juice together in an airtight jar; shake well.

- Toss red pepper, pear, and arugula together in a salad bowl; pour in dressing. Mix well then serve.

Nutrition Information

- Calories: 229 calories;

- Sodium: 159

- Total Carbohydrate: 13.8

- Cholesterol: 0

- Protein: 1.8

- Total Fat: 19.1

Cranberry Pecan Salad

Serving: 6

Ingredients

- 1 cup pecan halves

- 2 tablespoons raspberry vinegar

- 1/2 teaspoon Dijon mustard

- 1/2 teaspoon sugar

- 1/2 teaspoon salt

- freshly ground black pepper to taste (optional)

- 6 tablespoons olive oil

- 6 cups mixed salad greens, rinsed and dried

- 3/4 cup dried cranberries

- 1/2 medium red onion, thinly sliced

- crumbled feta cheese

Direction

- Set oven at 400°F (200°C) and start preheating. On a baking sheet, spread pecans evenly.

- Put pecans in the oven and toast for 8 to 10 minutes or until turn lightly brown and scented.

- Stir salt, pepper, sugar, mustard and vinegar together in a small bowl; mix well until salt and sugar dissolve fully in the liquid. Add in olive oil, whisk properly.

- Toss cheese, onions, pecans, cranberries and the greens together in a salad bowl. Pour in vinaigrette, toss lightly to coat salad with vinaigrette.

Nutrition Information

- Calories: 456 calories;

- Total Fat: 38.6

- Sodium: 780

- Total Carbohydrate: 21

- Cholesterol: 45

- Protein: 10

Cucumber Mango Salad With Citrus Vinaigrette

Serving: 4

Ingredients

- 1 English cucumber

- 1 mango

- 1 orange, juiced

- lemon, juiced

- 3 tablespoons grapefruit vinegar

- 4 leaves basil

- 1 pinch kosher salt

- 1 pinch ground black pepper

- 1/4 cup extra-virgin olive oil

Direction

- Remove cucumber skin. Use the vegetable peeler to peel strips of cucumber until you reach the soft core on all sides. Throw away cucumber core and skin. Put cucumber strips in a bowl.

- Remove mango skin. Use the vegetable peeler to peel strips of mango until you reach the seed on all sides. Throw away mango seed and skin. Put mango strips in the same bowl with cucumber.

- In a blender, combine black pepper, salt, basil, vinegar, lemon juice and orange juice, and puree. Slowly add in oil while blender is running. Pour dressing over cucumber and mango, mix well. Cover the bowl and keep cold for at least 2 hours

Nutrition Information

- Calories: 188 calories;
- Total Fat: 14.3
- Sodium: 103
- Total Carbohydrate: 17.2
- Cholesterol: 0
- Protein: 1.3

Dandelion Salad

Serving: 4

Ingredients

- 1/2 pound torn dandelion greens

- 1/2 red onion, chopped

- 2 tomatoes, chopped

- 1/2 teaspoon dried basil

- salt and pepper to taste

Direction

- Toss together tomatoes, red onion and dandelion greens in a medium bowl.

- Add salt, pepper and basil to taste.

Nutrition Information

- Calories: 42 calories;

- Sodium: 192

- Total Carbohydrate: 9

- Cholesterol: 0

- Protein: 2.3

- Total Fat: 0.5

Denise Salad Number One

Serving: 6

Ingredients

- 2 bunches arugula - rinsed, dried and torn
- 2 (11 ounce) cans mandarin orange segments, drained
- 1 large red onion, thinly sliced
- 1 pint cherry tomatoes
- 2 yellow bell peppers, seeded and diced
- 1 cup unsalted sunflower seeds
- 1/4 pound crumbled goat cheese
- 2 avocados - peeled, pitted and sliced

Direction

- Combine yellow peppers, tomatoes, onion, oranges and arugula in a large bowl. Choose your favorite dressing and add in the mixture. Add avocados, goat cheese and sunflower seeds on top then serve.

Nutrition Information

- Calories: 266 calories;

- Sodium: 136

- Total Carbohydrate: 26.2

- Cholesterol: 15

- Protein: 9.3

- Total Fat: 16.3

Detox Salad

Serving: 2

Ingredients

- 1 tablespoon cottage cheese

- 1 clove garlic, minced

- 1 teaspoon cider vinegar

- 1 tablespoon walnut oil

- salt and pepper to taste

- 2 Belgian endives, trimmed and leaves separated

- 1 apple, thinly sliced

- 1/2 cup stemmed watercress leaves

- 1/2 cup chopped walnuts

- 1/4 cup crumbled blue cheese

Direction

- In a small mixing bowl, mash together garlic and cottage cheese with a fork until smooth. Put in salt, pepper, walnut oil and cider vinegar, mix until well blended. Set aside.

- On two plates, lay out Belgian endive leaves in a circle as the tips point out. In the center of the plates, place apple, sprinkle with blue cheese, walnuts and watercress. Pour cottage cheese dressing over salads and serve.

Nutrition Information

- Calories: 370 calories;

- Total Fat: 30.9

- Sodium: 267

- Total Carbohydrate: 18.6

- Cholesterol: 13

- Protein: 9.9

Easy Arugula Salad

Serving: 4

Ingredients

- 4 cups young arugula leaves, rinsed and dried

- 1 cup cherry tomatoes, halved

- 1/4 cup pine nuts

- 2 tablespoons grapeseed oil or olive oil

- 1 tablespoon rice vinegar

- salt to taste

- freshly ground black pepper to taste

- 1/4 cup grated Parmesan cheese

- 1 large avocado - peeled, pitted and sliced

Direction

- Prepare a large plastic bowl that comes with a lid. In the bowl, combine Parmesan cheese, vinegar, oil, pine nuts, cherry tomatoes and arugula. Add salt and pepper to taste. Put the lid on to cover and shake until ingredients are well mixed.

- Separate salad onto plates, put avocado slices on top and serve

Nutrition Information

- Calories: 257 calories;

- Total Fat: 23.2

- Sodium: 381

- Total Carbohydrate: 10

- Cholesterol: 4

- Protein: 6.2

Green Apple Salad With Blueberries, Feta, And Walnuts

Serving: 4

Ingredients

- 4 cups mixed salad greens such as leaf lettuce, endive, and radicchio

- 1 large Granny Smith, cut into small cubes

- 1/2 cup chopped walnuts

- 1/2 cup crumbled feta cheese

- 1/2 cup dried cranberries

- 2 tablespoons finely chopped green onions (optional)

- Dressing:

- 1/4 cup vegetable oil

- 1/4 cup blueberries

- 2 tablespoons extra-virgin olive oil

- 2 tablespoons balsamic vinegar

- 1/4 teaspoon salt

Direction

- In a big bowl, put a layer of green onions, cranberries, feta cheese, walnuts, Granny smith apple, and salad greens.

- In a blender or a food processor, mix salt, balsamic vinegar, extra-virgin olive oil, blueberries, and vegetable oil together, pulse into a creamy dressing.

- Put the dressing on the salad, mix to coat. Refrigerate until ready to serve.

Nutrition Information

- Calories: 417 calories;

- Total Fat: 34.3

- Sodium: 372

- Total Carbohydrate: 26.1

Green Mango Salad

Serving: 4 | Prep: 30mins | Cook: | Ready in:

Ingredients

- 1 pound green mangoes - peeled, pitted, and cut into matchsticks
- 1/2 large red onion, thinly sliced
- 1 large ripe avocado, peeled and cut into wedges
- 2 tablespoons chopped dry-roasted peanuts
- 1 tablespoon soy sauce
- 1 tablespoon white sugar
- 1 tablespoon lime juice
- 1 teaspoon Thai pepper sauce
- 1 clove garlic

Direction

- In a large bowl, mix together peanuts, avocado, onion and mangoes

- In a small bowl, combine garlic, Thai pepper sauce, lime juice, sugar and soy sauce. Pour dressing over mango mixture. Stir properly until well coated

- Allow to sit at room temperature for 10 minutes in order that the flavors combined well then serve

Nutrition Information

- Calories: 236 calories;

- Sodium: 324

- Total Carbohydrate: 32.1

- Cholesterol: 0

- Protein: 3.5

- Total Fat: 12.8

Green Salad With Cranberry Vinaigrette

Serving: 8

Ingredients

- 1 cup sliced almonds
- 3 tablespoons red wine vinegar
- 1/3 cup olive oil
- 1/4 cup fresh cranberries
- 1 tablespoon Dijon mustard
- 1/2 teaspoon minced garlic
- 1/2 teaspoon salt
- 1/2 teaspoon ground black pepper
- 2 tablespoons water
- 1/2 red onion, thinly sliced
- 4 ounces crumbled blue cheese
- 1 pound mixed salad greens

Direction

- Preheat the oven to 190°C or 375°Fahrenheit. In a single layer, place almonds on a baking sheet. Toast almonds in the oven for five minutes until it starts to brown.

- Process water, vinegar, pepper, oil, salt, cranberries, garlic, and mustard in a food processor or blender until smooth.

- Mix greens, almonds, blue cheese, onion, and the vinegar mixture together in a large bowl until well coated.

Nutrition Information

- Calories: 218 calories;

- Total Carbohydrate: 6.2

- Cholesterol: 11

- Protein: 6.5

- Total Fat: 19.2

- Sodium: 405

Grilled Panzanella Salad With Peaches And Fennel

Serving: 4

Ingredients

- 1 large shallot, sliced thin

- 2 tablespoons white wine vinegar

- 1 teaspoon maple syrup (or sweetener of choice)

- 1/2 teaspoon fine sea salt and fresh pepper

- 6 tablespoons extra-virgin olive oil, divided

- 1 clove garlic

- 4 slices hearty bread

- 2 peaches, sliced into wedges

- 2 cups baby arugula

- 1 cup torn basil leaves

- 1 large fennel bulb, halved, cored and thinly shaved on a mandoline

- Reynolds Wrap® Non Stick Aluminum Foil

Direction

- Prepare Reynolds Wrap(R) Non Stick Aluminum Foil, cut a large piece and fit it firmly to the grill grate. Set the grill to medium heat

- While waiting the grill to heat, make the dressing. In a shallow bowl, add maple syrup, vinegar and shallot, season with a couple pinches of salt and pepper. Allow to sit for about 10 minutes until shallots become soft. Add in 4 tablespoon of the oil, whisk properly until dressing is blended and mixed. Set aside.

- Use a knife to cut garlic clove in half. Gently rub the cut side of the garlic to both sides of each slice of bread. Lightly glaze each side of the bread with 1 tablespoon of oil.

- Place bread on the heated grill and cook for about 7 to 10 minutes until bread becomes firm and toasted. Remove from the grill and allow to cool.

- Use the brush to glaze peaches with the remaining tablespoon of oil, season with a couple pinches of salt. On the foil-covered grill, place the peaches and cook for about 4 to 5 minutes until it turns light brown and firm. Remove from the heat and set aside.

- Mix together basil and arugula in a large serving bowl. Rip the bread in to large chunks, add into the bowl. Add in fennel and peaches. Add in the dressing, mix well then toss thoroughly

Nutrition Information

- Calories: 289 calories;
- Total Fat: 21.3
- Sodium: 410

- Total Carbohydrate: 21.7
- Cholesterol: 0
- Protein: 3.2

Grilled Romaine Salad

Serving: 8

Ingredients

1/2 cup olive oil

3 tablespoons white sugar

1 teaspoon dried rosemary

1 teaspoon dried thyme

1/4 teaspoon salt

1/4 teaspoon ground black pepper

8 Roma (plum) tomatoes, halved lengthwise

2 shallots, halved lengthwise and peeled

1/2 cup balsamic vinegar

2 tablespoons brown sugar

1 3/4 cups olive oil

4 romaine hearts

1 tablespoon olive oil

salt and pepper to taste

Direction

- Preheat the oven to 225°F (110°C). In a big Ziplock plastic bag, combine the thyme, olive oil, pepper, salt, rosemary and white sugar together. Put in the tomatoes then seal the Ziplock bag and shake well until fully coated. Place the coated halved tomatoes on a baking sheet, cut-side up. Put in the preheated oven and let it bake for 2 1/2 hours. Remove the tomatoes from the oven and allow it to cool down.

- Chop the shallots finely using a food processor or a blender. Put in the brown sugar and vinegar and blend until the consistency is smooth. While frequently blending, put in 1 3/4 cups of oil gradually until the mixture has thickened.

- Preheat the grill to high heat. Use a brush to coat the romaine hearts with 1 tablespoon of olive oil then sprinkle it with pepper and salt to taste.

- Put the seasoned romaine hearts onto the preheated grill. Let it cook on the grill for 5-10 minutes while turning it from time to time until the romaine hearts are burnt a little bit but not completely heated through. Serve it on salad plates while warm with the tomato pieces arranged around the salad; pour the shallot dressing on top.

Nutrition Information

- Calories: 622 calories;
- Total Fat: 62.8
- Sodium: 87
- Total Carbohydrate: 16.6
- Cholesterol: 0
- Protein: 1.5

Ham And Swiss Salad With Red Currants

Serving: 6

Ingredients

- 1 head romaine lettuce, rinsed, patted dry and chopped
- 4 ounces arugula, washed and dried
- 4 ounces sliced mushrooms
- 1 cup grape tomatoes, halved
- 1 shallot, thinly sliced
- 1 cup fresh red currants
- 1/2 cup shredded Swiss cheese
- 4 ounces honey ham, chopped
- 1/4 cup balsamic vinegar
- 1/4 cup extra virgin olive oil
- salt and pepper to taste

Direction

- In a large salad bowl, mix together ham, Swiss cheese, currants, shallot, tomatoes, mushrooms, arugula and romaine.

- In a small bowl, put in salt and pepper, olive oil and balsamic vinegar, whisk until mixed well. Pour the dressing over the salad and toss until well coated.

Nutrition Information

- Calories: 187 calories;

- Total Fat: 12.8

- Sodium: 188

- Total Carbohydrate: 11.3

- Cholesterol: 18

- Protein: 8.1

Hot Chicken Liver And Fennel Salad

Serving: 4

Ingredients

- 4 cups spinach, rinsed and chopped
- 1 bulb fennel - trimmed, quartered and sliced
- 2 tablespoons butter
- 1/4 cup olive oil
- 2 cloves garlic, minced
- 1 pound chicken livers, trimmed and sliced
- 1/2 cup chicken broth
- 1 teaspoon capers, chopped
- 4 anchovy filets, rinsed and chopped
- 1 teaspoon dried sage

- 1/2 teaspoon salt

- 1/4 teaspoon ground black pepper

Direction

- Separate spinach into 4 salad plates

- Melt 1 tablespoon butter in a large deep skillet over medium heat; add in fennel, cook for about 3 minutes or until it becomes soft. Remove fennel from skillet, set aside

- Heat olive oil with remaining butter in the same skillet; add in garlic, cook for 1 minute. Add in chicken livers; cook for 3 to 4 minutes or until the liver is no longer pink in the center.

- Return cooked fennel to skillet. Add in salt and pepper, sage, carpers, anchovies and stock; cook the mixture over high heat for 2 to 3 minutes or until the amount of sauce is slightly decreased

- Add a spoon of mixture over each salad dish and decorate with fennel leaves. Serve immediately

Nutrition Information

- Calories: 348 calories;

- Cholesterol: 411

- Protein: 23.5

- Total Fat: 25.7

- Sodium: 831

- Total Carbohydrate: 6.3

Jarjeer (Arugula) Salad

Serving: 4

Ingredients

- 1 bunch arugula

- 2 onions, thinly sliced

- 1 cup chopped mushrooms

- 1 tomato, diced (optional)

- 1 teaspoon extra virgin olive oil

- 1/2 lemon, juiced

- 2 teaspoons sumac (see Note)

- Salt to taste

Direction

- Wash arugula leaves and then dry.

- Spread the leaves onto a large plate and then spread a layer of tomato, onions, and mushrooms.

- Whisk sumac, olive oil, and lemon juice together.

- Add salt to taste and spread atop the salad.

Nutrition Information

- Calories: 62 calories;

- Protein: 3.2

- Total Fat: 1.8

- Sodium: 22

- Total Carbohydrate: 10.4

- Cholesterol: 0

Eggplant Salad With Feta And Pomegranate

Serving: 4

Ingredients

- 2 eggplants, sliced
- 1 tablespoon salt, divided
- 1 cup yogurt
- 1 lemon, juiced
- 2 tablespoons olive oil
- 1 teaspoon ground black pepper
- 2 tomatoes, chopped
- 1 cucumber, chopped
- 1 pomegranate, seeds only
- 1/4 cup feta cheese

Direction

- Set an outdoor grill to medium heat and start preheating, lightly glaze the grate with oil.

Sprinkle eggplant slices with 1/2 tablespoon salt to season.

- Cook eggplant on preheated oven for 10 to 15 minutes or until it becomes soft, remember to flip halfway through. Move to a platter and layout eggplant in a single layer.

- In a bowl, put black pepper, remaining 1/2 tablespoon salt, olive oil, lemon juice and yogurt, whisk well.

- Pour yogurt dressing on top of eggplant. Add cucumber and tomatoes on top. Sprinkle on top with feta cheese and pomegranate seeds.

Nutrition Information

- Calories: 284 calories;

- Total Carbohydrate: 41.5

- Cholesterol: 18

- Protein: 10.4

- Total Fat: 12.1

Elegant Brunch Chicken Salad

Serving: 6

Ingredients

- 1 pound skinless, boneless chicken breast halves
- 1 egg
- 1/4 teaspoon dry mustard
- 1/2 teaspoon salt
- 2 teaspoons hot water
- 1 tablespoon white wine vinegar
- 1 cup olive oil
- 2 cups halved seedless red grapes
- 1 cup coarsely chopped pecans
- 1 cup coarsely crumbled blue cheese

Direction

- In a large pot, put in water and bring to a boil. Add in chicken and simmer for approximately 10 minutes until cooked well. Drain the chicken, let it cool and cut into cubes

- When chicken is boiling, make mayonnaise: Prepare a hand-held electric mixer or blender, use it to beat vinegar, water, salt, mustard and egg together until frothy and light. Add in one tablespoon of oil at a time, after each tablespoon of oil, beat thoroughly. When mixture starts to thickened, you can add oil more frequently. Continue to beat until mixture achieves the consistent and creamy texture of a mayonnaise.

- NOTE: The thickness of mayonnaise depends on the amount of oil you put in, it will get thicker if you add more oil; the full cup of oil might not be necessary

- Mix together 1 cup of homemade mayonnaise, blue cheese, pecans, grapes and chicken in a large bowl. Stir until salad is coated evenly, add more mayonnaise if needed. Keep cold until serving

Nutrition Information

- Calories: 657 calories;
- Total Carbohydrate: 12.6
- Cholesterol: 92
- Protein: 25.4
- Total Fat: 57.7
- Sodium: 571

Roasted Vegetable Salad

Serving: 10

Ingredients

- 1 eggplant - quartered lengthwise, and sliced into 1/2 inch pieces

- 2 small yellow squash, halved lengthwise and sliced

- 4 cloves garlic, peeled

- 1/4 cup olive oil, or as needed

- 1 red bell pepper, seeded and sliced into strips

- 1 bunch fresh asparagus, trimmed and cut into 2 inch pieces

- 1/2 red onion, sliced

- 1/4 cup red wine vinegar

- 2 tablespoons balsamic vinegar

- 1/4 cup olive oil

- 2 lemons, juiced

- 1/4 cup chopped fresh parsley

- 3 tablespoons chopped fresh oregano

- salt and freshly ground black pepper to taste

Direction

- Set an oven to 450°C (230°F). Grease a large baking sheet.

- On the prepared baking sheet, evenly lay out eggplant and quash slices in layer. Place garlic cloves in one side of the pan so they can be found easily later. Bake in the preheated oven for 15 minutes.

- While roasting the vegetables, put lemon juice, olive oil, balsamic vinegar and red wine vinegar together in a large serving bowl, whisk until well combined. Add salt, pepper, parsley and oregano to season. Remove cloves of garlic from the oven and mash or chop into smaller pieces. Add garlic to dressing, whisk well and set aside.

- Remove vegetables from the oven, and stir the eggplant and the squash well. Place asparagus, red onion and red bell pepper in layer on top of squash and eggplant. Put back in the oven and bake for an additional 15 to 20 minutes or until asparagus becomes soft but still has bright green color.

- Remove them from oven once vegetables are cooked well and slightly toasted. Place them in a bowl, pour in dressing, and stir until evenly coated. Taste and adjust the amount of salt and pepper if needed. Allow to chill for a few hours to marinate the vegetables.

Nutrition Information

Calories: 139 calories;

Total Carbohydrate: 10.8

Cholesterol: 0

Protein: 2.4

Total Fat: 11.2

Sodium: 64

Ensalada De Nopales (Mexican Cactus Salad)

Serving: 4

Ingredients

2 nopales (cactus pads)

3 tablespoons olive oil, divided

salt and ground black pepper to taste

4 Roma tomatoes, thinly sliced

2 serrano chiles, thinly sliced

1/2 cup thinly sliced pickled red onion, or to taste

1 lime, juiced

2 tablespoons finely chopped cilantro

1 teaspoon dried oregano

2 tablespoons cotija cheese

2 avocados, halved and pitted

2 tablespoons roasted sesame seeds

Direction

- Set an outdoor grill to medium heat and start preheating. Glaze the grate lightly with oil.

- Use a brush to glaze 1 tablespoon of oil on both sides of nopales. Sprinkle with salt and pepper to taste. Place on the preheated grill and cook, flipping half way through, for 7 to 9 minutes or until nopales become soft. Remove from grill and allow it to cool until safe to handle. Cut nopales into 1/2 inch strips.

- On a serving plate, place onion, serrano chiles and tomatoes in layers. Place grilled nopales on top of vegetables bed; sprinkle salad with remaining 2 tablespoons oil and lime juice. Add oregano and cilantro on top. Put in cotija cheese.

- Cut each avocado half without removing the skin; gently scoop sliced avocado on top of the salad in a fan shape using a spoon. Add sesame seeds and additional salt and pepper on top.

Nutrition Information

- Calories: 335 calories;
- Total Carbohydrate: 17.4
- Cholesterol: 7
- Protein: 5.5
- Total Fat: 29.5
- Sodium: 844

Escarole Siciliano

Serving: 3

Ingredients

- 3 tablespoons olive oil
- 2 medium heads escarole - rinsed, dried and chopped
- 1/2 cup lemon juice
- 2 tablespoons capers
- 1 pinch salt
- 10 kalamata olives
- ground black pepper to taste

Direction

- In a wok, heat oil over high heat. Put in escarole; cook and stir until greens turn wilted.
- Add lemon juice, stir well. Add olives, salt and carpers; cook and stir well for another 15 seconds.

Add salt and black pepper to season. Serve immediately.

Nutrition Information

- Calories: 224 calories;
- Cholesterol: 0
- Protein: 4.8
- Total Fat: 17.5
- Sodium: 450
- Total Carbohydrate: 16.4

Fall Salad With Quinoa, Brussels Sprouts, And Pomegranate

Serving: 4

Ingredients

- 1 tablespoon butter

- 1 1/2 cups quinoa, rinsed and drained

- 1 1/2 cups vegetable broth

- 3 cups roughly chopped Brussels sprouts

- 6 tablespoons olive oil, divided

- salt and ground black pepper to taste

- 1/3 cup white wine vinegar

- 1/4 cup honey

- 2 tablespoons Dijon mustard

- 1 clove garlic, minced

- 1 pinch herbes de Provence, or to taste

- 4 cups arugula

- 1 1/4 cups pomegranate seeds

- 1/3 cup roasted and salted shelled pistachios

- 1/2 cup crumbled goat cheese

- 4 slices multigrain bread, toasted

Direction

- Let butter melt over medium-high heat in a small pot. Toss in quinoa and sauté for 1-3 minutes, until quinoa starts to pop and brown. Pour in broth. Put lid on. Lower the heat to low. Let it simmer for 25-minutes, until all the water is gone.

- Set the oven to preheat at 400F (200C). Prepare a baking sheet with parchment paper.

- Meanwhile, arrange the Brussel sprouts on the baking sheet. Drizzle 2 tablespoons of olive oil on. Sprinkle on salt and pepper. Toss to coat well.

- Roast the Brussel sprouts for 15-20 minutes in the oven, until brown and cooked through but still firm.

- Combine remaining olive oil, honey, vinegar, mustard, salt, pepper, garlic, and herbes de Provence in a bowl.
- Mix the roasted Brussel sprouts, cooked quinoa, pistachios, and dressing in a bowl. Toss in 2/3 of the pomegranate seeds, 2/3 of goat cheese, and arugula. Mix gently.
- Divide into 4 portions. Top with the rest of the goat cheese and pomegranate seeds. Pair each serving with a slice of toasted bread.

Nutrition Information

- Calories: 764 calories;
- Total Carbohydrate: 91.4
- Cholesterol: 24
- Total Fat: 38.3
- Protein: 20.8
- Sodium: 702

Fennel And Orange Salad

Serving: 4

Ingredients

- 1 bulb fennel, trimmed and sliced
- 2 large oranges, sliced into rounds
- 1 tablespoon olive oil
- 1 tablespoon red wine vinegar
- 1 teaspoon poppy seeds
- salt to taste
- 2 bunches arugula - rinsed, dried and chopped

Direction

- In a large bowl, place in fennel and orange. Add in vinegar and olive oil; drizzle salt and poppyseeds.

- Allow to chill, put mixture over a bed of arugula and serve

Nutrition Information

- Calories: 128 calories;
- Total Fat: 4.7
- Sodium: 65
- Total Carbohydrate: 20.2
- Cholesterol: 0
- Protein: 4.9

French Lentil Salad With Goat Cheese

Serving: 4

Ingredients

- 3 tablespoons sherry vinegar
- 3 tablespoons olive oil
- 1/2 teaspoon minced garlic
- 1 tablespoon olive oil
- 1 cup French green lentils
- 1 (14.5 ounce) can chicken broth
- 1 cup water
- 1/3 cup chopped fresh chives
- 1/4 cup chopped fresh cilantro
- 1/2 cup crumbled chevre (goat cheese)
- 1/2 cup quartered grape tomatoes (optional)

Direction

- In a jar that comes with a lid, combine minced garlic, 3 tablespoons olive oil and sherry vinegar in the jar, cover and shake until ingredients are well blended. Set aside.

- In a saucepan, place 1 tablespoon of olive oil, water, chicken broth and lentils, bring mixture to a boil. Cover saucepan with lid, lower the heat to low and simmer for about 20 minutes or until lentils are soft to the bite. Remember not to overcook. Remove from the heat, drain off water and allow it to cool for a minimum of 30 minutes. Move cooled lentils to a mixing bowl.

- Add cilantro, chives and the dressing, stir until well mixed. If the salad needs to be served right away, put in tomatoes and goat cheese. If not, keep salad in the refrigerator and put in tomatoes and goat cheese right before serving.

Nutrition Information

- Calories: 329 calories;

- Protein: 14.7

- Total Fat: 19.5

- Sodium: 533

- Total Carbohydrate: 24.9

- Cholesterol: 16

Fresh Avocado Burrata Salad

Serving: 4

Ingredients

- 1 (5 ounce) package baby arugula

- 4 ounces prosciutto, torn into small pieces

- 1/4 cup olive oil

- 1 tablespoon balsamic vinegar

- 1 (4 ounce) ball burrata cheese

- 1 large avocado - peeled, pitted, and sliced

- 1 small Roma tomato, diced

- salt and ground black pepper to taste

Direction

- In a bowl, toss together balsamic vinegar, olive oil, prosciutto and baby arugula. Use tongs to move mixture to a large serving plate. Put a ball of burrata cheese in the center. Lay out avocado slices around the plate and place tomato on top. Drizzle with salt and ground black pepper.
- Quarter burrata cheese and distribute salad into 4 plates to serve.

Nutrition Information

Calories: 431 calories;

Total Carbohydrate: 8.4

Cholesterol: 45

Protein: 11.9

Total Fat: 39.2

Sodium: 674

Gabe's Coffee Crusted Hanger Steak With Apple, Fennel, And Herb Salad

Serving: 4

Ingredients

- Coffee Chile Spice Rub:

- 1 tablespoon fennel seeds

- 1 tablespoon cumin seeds

- 1 tablespoon coriander seeds

- 1/4 cup finely ground dark roast coffee beans

- 1/4 cup ground ancho chile pepper

- 1/4 cup brown sugar

- 2 1/2 tablespoons kosher salt

- 2 tablespoons hot smoked paprika

- 2 teaspoons ground black pepper
- 2 teaspoons red pepper flakes
- Steak:
- 1 pound hanger steak
- salt to taste
- 1 teaspoon olive oil
- 4 shallots, halved
- 3 cloves garlic, smashed
- 3 sprigs fresh thyme
- 1 tablespoon butter, cut in small pieces
- Salad Dressing:
- 1 lemon, zested and juiced
- 1 tablespoon olive oil
- 2 teaspoons honey
- salt and ground black pepper to taste
- Salad:
- 1 bulb fennel, halved

- 1/2 lemon, juiced

- 1/2 apple, cut into matchstick-size pieces

- 1 tablespoon fresh mint leaves, or to taste

- 1 tablespoon fresh parsley leaves, or to taste

- 1 tablespoon fresh cilantro leaves, or to taste

- 1/4 cup pomegranate seeds

- 2 tablespoons chopped hazelnuts

Direction

- In a skillet over medium-high heat, put in coriander seeds, cumin seeds and fennel seeds, cook and stir for 1 to 2 minutes until toasted and scented. Move to a food processor or spice grinder; add in red pepper flakes, black pepper, paprika, kosher salt, brown sugar, ancho chile pepper and coffee. Grind until spice rub mixture achieves a medium-coarse texture.

- Cut steak into 4-ounce pieces. Use a knife to lightly score steak into 1/2 inch-1/2 inch. Add salt to season. Use spice rub to rub the steak. Set to medium-high and start heating a cast iron skillet. Make sure the spice rub is packed onto all sides of the steak, place the steak in the hot cast iron skillet; pour about 1 teaspoon of olive oil over steak.

- Cook steak for about 4 minutes until well browned in the cast iron skillet. Turn the steak over and scatter butter, thyme, smashed garlic and shallots in the skillet around steak. Cook for 4 to 5 minutes more until steak reaches the doneness you want. Use an instant-read thermometer to measure the temperature of steak, it should be inserted in the middle and read at least 140°F (60°C). Allow steak to rest for 5 minutes then cut it into thin slices.

- In a small bowl, whisk together salt, pepper, honey, olive oil, lemon zest and juice of 1 lemon until mixed evenly.

- In a bowl, add in thinly shave fennel and juice of 1/2 lemon, toss well to preserve color. Add cilantro, parsley, mint and apple. Pour dressing over salad, mixed gently until well coated; add salt and pepper to season. Place steak slices on

top of salad and scatter hazelnuts,
pomegranate seeds and roasted shallots on top.

Nutrition Information

- Calories: 413 calories;

- Sodium: 3782

- Total Carbohydrate: 53.9

- Cholesterol: 33

- Protein: 20.7

- Total Fat: 17.1

Mango Papaya Salad

Serving: 6

Ingredients

- 1 large mango - peeled, seeded and halved
- 1 medium papaya - peeled, seeded and halved
- 1 avocado - peeled, pitted and diced
- 3 tablespoons balsamic vinegar
- 1 tablespoon butter
- 1/4 cup blanched slivered almonds
- 1 teaspoon brown sugar
- 1 head romaine lettuce, torn into bite-size pieces
- salt to taste

Direction

- Put half of the papaya and half of the mango into the container of a blender or food processor together with balsamic vinegar. Blend until it turns smooth, and reserve.

- Put butter in a small skillet to melt on medium heat. Put in almonds and cook stirring continuously until lightly browned. Mix in brown sugar and stir to coat. Separate from heat, and place candied almonds onto a piece of waxed paper, getting rid of any clumps. Reserve to cool.

- Just prior to serving, put romaine lettuce in a large serving bowl. Then cube leftover papaya halves and mango, and gently toss with lettuce and avocado. Drizzle on the pureed fruit over the salad and lightly salt. Sprinkle with candied almonds, and serve right away.

Nutrition Information

- Calories: 148 calories;

- Total Carbohydrate: 16

- Cholesterol: 5

- Protein: 2.7

- Total Fat: 9.4

- Sodium: 25

Mandarin Orange Salad

Serving: 6

Ingredients

- Dressing

- 1 onion, minced

- 2/3 cup white sugar

- 1 tablespoon dry mustard

- 1 teaspoon celery seed

- 1 teaspoon black pepper

- 1/2 cup distilled white vinegar

- 1/2 cup olive oil

- Salad

- 1 head romaine lettuce, chopped

- 1 (10 ounce) can mandarin oranges, drained

- 5 ounces fresh mushrooms, sliced

- 3 tablespoons slivered almonds

- 3 tablespoons crumbled cooked bacon

Direction

- In a small bowl, place black pepper, celery seed, mustard, sugar and onion. Stir in vinegar to dissolve the sugar. Add olive oil and whisk till the dressing is thickened. Cover and store for at least 3 hours in the fridge.

- For the salad, in a large bowl, toss bacon, almonds, mushrooms, oranges and lettuce together. Drizzle dressing over and toss again till coated.

Nutrition Information

- Calories: 332 calories;

- Sodium: 120

- Total Carbohydrate: 34.1

- Cholesterol: 2

- Protein: 4.6

- Total Fat: 21.2

Gourmet Tuna Salad

Serving: 4

Ingredients

- 1 (12 ounce) can albacore tuna in water, drained and flaked

- 2 green onions, chopped

- 1 stalk celery, diced

- 1/4 cup pimento-stuffed green olives, chopped

- 2 tablespoons capers, chopped

- 1/4 cup blanched slivered almonds

- 1 dash Worcestershire sauce

- 1/2 cup mayonnaise

- 1/4 cup sour cream

Direction

- Combine almonds, capers, green olives, celery, green onions and tuna in a mixing bowl

- Whisk together Worcestershire sauce, sour cream and mayonnaise in a small bowl

- Mix together tuna mixture and dressing. Place mixture over bed of lettuce or with croissant as a tuna salad sandwich, and serve

Nutrition Information

- Calories: 396 calories;

- Total Fat: 32.4

- Sodium: 908

- Total Carbohydrate: 4.1

- Cholesterol: 52

- Protein: 22.5

Calamari Salad

Serving: 12

Ingredients

2 lemons, juiced

6 cloves garlic, peeled and minced

1 sprig fresh parsley, chopped

salt and pepper to taste

3 pounds squid, cleaned and sliced into rounds

1 (2.25 ounce) can pitted black olives

4 stalks celery, chopped

Direction

- Mix parsley, garlic, and lemon juice in a medium bowl. Season with pepper and salt.

- Boil a medium pot of water. Mix in squid. Cook until tender for about 3 minutes. Drain.

- Toss lemon juice mixture, celery, olives, and squid. Cover and keep in fridge to chill. Serve.

Nutrition Information

- Calories: 119 calories;
- Cholesterol: 264
- Protein: 18.2
- Total Fat: 2.2
- Sodium: 108
- Total Carbohydrate: 6.8

Greek Pasta Salad With Roasted Vegetables And Feta

Serving: 6

Ingredients

- 1 red bell pepper, cut into 1/2 inch pieces
- 1 yellow bell pepper, chopped
- 1 medium eggplant, cubed
- 3 small yellow squash, cut in 1/4 inch slices
- 6 tablespoons extra virgin olive oil
- 1/4 teaspoon salt
- 1/4 teaspoon ground black pepper
- 1 1/2 ounces sun-dried tomatoes, soaked in 1/2 cup boiling water
- 1/2 cup torn arugula leaves
- 1/2 cup chopped fresh basil
- 2 tablespoons balsamic vinegar
- 2 tablespoons minced garlic

- 4 ounces crumbled feta cheese
- 1 (12 ounce) package farfalle pasta

Direction

- Preheat oven to 230°C/450°F. Line foil on cookie sheet; spray using nonstick cooking spray.

- Toss 2 tbsp. olive oil, pepper, salt, squash, eggplant, and yellow and red bell pepper in medium bowl. Put on prepped cookie sheet.

- In preheated oven, bake veggies for 25 minutes till lightly browned, occasionally tossing.

- Cook pasta in big pot with salted boiling water till al dente for 10-12 minutes; drain.

- Drain softened sun-dried tomatoes; keep water. Toss basil, arugula, sun-drained tomatoes, cooked pasta and roasted veggies in big bowl. Mix feta cheese, garlic, balsamic vinegar, reserved water from tomatoes and leftover olive oil in. Toss till coated. Season to taste with pepper and salt; immediately serve or refrigerate till chilled.

Nutrition Information

- Calories: 446 calories;

- Protein: 13.8

- Total Fat: 19.5

- Sodium: 324

- Total Carbohydrate: 56.9

- Cholesterol: 17

THANK YOU

Thank you for choosing *Cooking Salads for Beginners* for improving your cooking skills! I hope you enjoyed making the recipes as much as tasting them! If you're interested in learning new recipes and new meals to cook, go and check out the other books of the series.

CPSIA information can be obtained
at www.ICGtesting.com
Printed in the USA
BVHW080738140521
607270BV00005B/673